EMPLOYEE
ENGAGEMENT

20 keys to an outstanding Workplace Communication

ANTONI LACINAI

EMPLOYEE ENGAGEMENT
20 keys to an outstanding
Workplace Communication

Layout: Pia Lilenthal
Illustrations: Antoni Lacinai
Publisher: Lacinai AB
ISBN: 978-91-519-4234-6

PREVIOUS BOOKS IN ENGLISH
BY ANTONI LACINAI

Understanding Body Language.
BoD. 2016

Make meetings work.
BoD. 2016

Virtual meetings. Set them up. Lead them well. Reach your goal.
BoD. 2017

TABLE OF

PART 1 – SEVEN UNIVERSAL TRUTHS

contents

COMMUNICATION BETWEEN PEOPLE
IS LIKE ELECTRICITY
IN A MODERN SOCIETY.

WITHOUT IT WE DIE!

"HEY YOU!"

*I*t was a warm summer night in the early 90's. I made my way up a long hill towards my apartment in downtown Gothenburg. Two younger guys stopped me.

"Hey, you!" said one of them. *"Do you have a cigarette?"*

"No," I said, trying to move on. I was stopped again.

"Give us your wallet!" said the other guy.

"No!" I said. The first one stuck his hand inside his thin jacket and brought out a gun.

"Are you sure about that?" he asked.

"No," I said, giving them my wallet.

After 10-15 seconds of debating between them, to my surprise, I got it back.

"It's cool. You can take it back. You had such good answers to our questions," they said.

> ### *In my head a single word echoed ... ("No!")*

But I didn't say it out loud. Instead, I pretended to be their friend and we talked for a while.

After a few minutes, we parted ways. I went home, came into my apartment and sat on the edge of the bed. There it hit me; I could have been dead by now! I wasn't dead, injured or even robbed. How could that be?

From that moment on, I went from being interested in communication to being passionate about it. Since then I have been searching for the keys to great communication…

THE MYSTERIES OF
communication...

We all want to be seen, heard, understood, respected. This rarely happens. Everyone is so busy with themselves, there is little energy left to focus on others. The biggest mystery of communication is that many people somehow believe that they master it. This is what I call humor – a joke. We think that, just because we learned words and sentences at a young age, we are Jedi Masters of Communication. We are not.

We have always communicated. First with body language and grunts. Then with words and writing. Today it is on social media that we broadcast our every thought. But who's listening? Have we improved the quality just because we've increased the quantity?

We also see a really low level of engagement in the workplace, according to Gallup surveys. For too many people, going to work is, at best, a neutral experience, a way to make a living. To some people it is far worse. It doesn't have to be that way. We could do so much better.

This is where you and I come into the picture! We will make a positive difference – together. We will see people, welcome them, listen to them and invest in them – so our workplaces become magnets to people. They'll want to be there and contribute. We'll do this together. This is my mission. Will you join me?

...are nothing less than
A MATTER OF LIFE AND DEATH

Since before history, we humans needed to cooperate to survive, and we became quite good at it. Today we may not die just because we lack some communication skills, but it can create misunderstanding, irritation, anger, sadness, gossip, bullying and other miseries.

Great communication creates motivation, inspiration, meaning, joy, patience, endurance and a better performance. We want to be in that space, context and workplace!

In this book you will get my 20 truths about workplace communication. You can call them keys, principles, secrets, lessons or success factors. They are simple, effective tips and thoughts that can strengthen you in your relationships with colleagues, managers, employees and others. Some are based on years of observation. Much is backed up with sources from psychology and similar research. Email me if you want an incomplete list of sources on antoni@lacinai.se

Beware: My own experience is that it can easily backfire if you use your family as test subjects...

THE *three* SUPERPOWERS OF COMMUNICATION

*I*f you want to be a great leader, colleague, customer, supplier and fellow human being, you also want to be a great communicator. At work we want to have fun. We want to collaborate and perform together. We want to get along with our colleagues. If you are good at communicating, you will have more influence, and influence is the very definition of leadership.

There are three superpowers that make you a person of influence.

ENERGY so we can believe that you believe. Why should we if you don't? Energy is mostly shown in your body language and in your voice. If you show us your spirit, your passion, your determination and your joy, we will follow you.

EMPATHY so we feel that you understand us. We want to feel noticed and recognized. We want you to listen. Empathy creates trust and we will follow you if we trust you.

CLARITY so that you remove as many misunderstandings as possible. If you explain things in a clear way, we will understand things easier and that will make us feel smart – and we follow anyone who makes us feel smart.

These three superpowers are the essence of all 20 communication truths that will follow.

YOU ARE LISTENING TO *WII FM*

*T*he rest of the book is split into two parts. The first seven keys are universal, generic thoughts that will, hopefully, make you think. The next thirteen are more concrete tips that you can try in your everyday life right away. That being said, my goal is that everything I offer you should be something you can use, now or someday soon.

After each key, or truth, you'll get three questions to reflect upon. Why not do it? Maybe you'll make this book your 20-week program? Maybe you'll highlight one truth at a time at your internal meetings and discuss how it might help you? Maybe you'll speed-read until something catches your eye?

I learned a long time ago that everyone is tapping into the same radio channel in meetings with others:

WII FM – What's In It For Me?

Think about it. What does all this mean for you personally? For you as a team? Is it true or is it just bogus? How can you get more job satisfaction and motivation with the help of these keys? What do you need to do?

You choose. You decide.

PART 1

7 UNIVERSAL TRUTHS

1. YOU CANNOT *not*

COMMUNICATE

Have you ever gone into a store where two clerks are talking to each other and ignoring you completely? How did that make you feel? Did they communicate with you? Of course they did! They told you that you're not important. Communication is not only what you say. It is:

- What you think.
- What you say.
- What you DO.

You cannot choose whether or not you communicate. Everything about you communicates. What you say, how you sound, what you do, what you don't do, the clothes you wear, your hairstyle, how you get to work, what you eat for lunch, who you look at and who you don't look at.

Imagine you're the boss and you are in a meeting. You find it boring and decide to be efficient, so you pick up you phone and respond to some emails. This will not go unnoticed. Your people will think *"Hm, we're obviously less important than whatever is on that screen..."*

Fruit baskets
AND BUSINESS CLASS

In 2001, the telecom industry was in deep crisis. Over a period of three years, the company I was working at was to lay off half its 110,000 employees. Amputation was the only way for the company to survive. In the first cycle, 80 percent of my colleagues in the department had to hand in their access cards and go home. Those were tough times.

I have many memories from that period. Some good. Others really bad.

In my business unit there was a manager who, every day at the same time, met with us on the same open space on the same floor in our building. Those who wanted could go there and listen to the latest news and ask questions. Often, he had nothing new to say, but the fact that he stood there, instead of hiding, communicated plenty. I admired him for that.

That was one of the good memories.
Now to some ...well, not so great:

We used to have fruit baskets in every department. They were removed. It was to some extent a symbolic act, but we got the message. Also, no trips were allowed except the absolutely necessary ones. We got that message too.

But then two things happened in a short time that irritated us employees. First, we discovered that the fruit baskets on the executive floor were still there. Strange. Shouldn't we all pull our weight? Did they need fruit more than we did because their thoughts required more energy than ours?

Then several of us were assigned to fly to France and work in an important trade show. Of course, we booked tickets in economy class. But as we stepped onto the plane, some of the higher managers sat in business class at the front of the plane. We were surprised. Didn't we have a crisis in the company? The managers quickly got very busy reading something on their computers or the menus from their seat pockets. No one looked at us as we paraded by. They knew that we knew, and they were more than a little embarrassed. At the same time, back at base, staff were being dismissed. It all felt absurd.

Everything and everyone communicate – always.
Believe it!

Reflect on this:

Do you say "Good morning" to each other when you arrive at work?

How would you like to be described?

What are your fruit baskets?

"I DON'T LISTEN TO WHAT THE BOSS SAYS
I LISTEN TO WHAT THE BOSS DOES!"
— KJELL DAHLIN

2. YOU MAKE PEOPLE *feel*

WHAT YOU WANT THEM TO *feel*

*I*f you threaten me, I get scared. If you praise me, I get happy. If you show me 58 PowerPoint slides filled with text, I get sleepy…

What you think, say and do will affect not only your mood but also everyone else's. And it doesn't stop there. The way we feel will then affect our performance. This is an important insight since it connects communication, employee engagement and results!

A smile. A thought. A word. Everything affects people – more than you think. If you wake up in the morning with an inner voice that says

Nnnnn o o o o o o

then it's obviously not good to try building a constructive dialogue with you until you have had a few cups of coffee.

According to experts, three to eleven positive interactions are required for each negative interaction to create a high-performing team. Praise each other. Find the joy. It is really important. Speaking of praise: It is said that half of all the praise you get through life you get before you turn three years old…

Your power is greater than you might think. Use it wisely. Fill your life with good thoughts, words and actions. For you and for the people around you.

THE BOSS'S *communication* SETS THE CULTURE

A few years ago, I was given the assignment to train 18 salespeople at a large IT distributor for three hours. The topic was how to communicate and perform in their booth at a trade show. I got a little worried when I couldn't get hold of the sales manager in advance. I called him, left messages, emailed…He did not respond. "He must be extremely busy," I thought.

Once I got there, only 12 of the 18 salespeople showed up. Perhaps they had an emergency? Yet the sales manager was there and he seemed calm – sitting apart from the others, setting up his laptop and getting stuck into his e-mails. As I recall, he didn't welcome me or introduce me to the team. That was strange…but still ok.

So I started by introducing myself, the purpose and the topics of the three hours. So far so good. Then I said,

> *"Since we only have three hours, it would be good if you could put your phones in flight mode – switch them to silent"*

The sales manager looked up for the first time and exclaimed in a loud voice:

My authority and mandate went out the window. Half of the gang immediately began to fiddle with their phones. During a short break, those people disappeared for good. Six ambitious salespeople remained the whole time. Guess who performed best at the exhibition?

I once read this in a study: Of 55 factors determining an employee's engagement – 37 depend on the manager's behavior! The immediate boss affects more people, more strongly, than others do. They look at him/her and copy what he/she is doing. This is how a culture is created.

This was one of the hardest experiences I've had in my life as a consultant. Recently I got an email from that same company. A newcomer to their marketing department asked me if I could train their stand staff. She didn't know the history. I called her up and said "I am willing to train your staff, unless the same sales manager is around." She said she would to get back to me. I haven't heard anything and I am not sad about it.

Reflect on this:

How affected are you by what other people do or say?

When was the last time you helped somebody without being asked or ordered to?

How much do you praise each other? Can you do more?

FEELINGS ARE CONTAGIOUS.
CHOOSE WISELY HOW YOU
LEAN YOUR HEAD) :)

SOME FOLKS ARE
CONSTANTLY GRUMPY.
THEY DRAG YOU DOWN,
SO THAT THEY CAN FEEL
BETTER IN COMPARISON.

THEY ARE VAMPIRES!

EAT PLENTY OF GARLIC IF YOU
HAVE A MEETING WITH THEM.

3. YOU CANNOT *say* WHAT

YOU MEAN

*I'*m sorry, but you can't. Your brain is not a computer with linear algorithms and ones and zeros in a serial flow. Your brain is a crow's nest, a mess…and not just a mess, it's your mess. What comes out is not exactly what you mean. The content has passed several filters of experiences, prejudices, generalizations and omissions. What's left is something that – you hope – is close enough to your original intention.

But wait, it gets worse.

You don't even own your content once it's out. Everyone else does. Your words will pass through their respective filters too, which will make each of them remember different parts of your message.

This connects directly to the communicative superpower Clarity, mentioned before. It isn't easy to be clear. In fact, the more I study communication, the more baffled I am that we understand each other at all! It shouldn't be possible. Sometimes, when I give a lecture, I say to the audience: *"Hands up if you misunderstood someone this past week."* Most people raise their hand. Those who don't have obviously misunderstood the question…

THAT'S *not* WHAT I MEANT

*I*was at a project meeting with a customer before a big event. There were about ten of us, and the atmosphere was positive, even though everyone was on their toes and a bit nervous. Then I said something really bad:

"I understand that it has all escalated now."

The answer came fast from one of the people I had not met before.

"Nothing has escalated here. We can make our own decisions, thank you very much!! "

"Oh, no!" I thought, as I realized my mistake. In the client's home language, "escalate" meant referring the decision upwards in the hierarchy. I had just told this guy that he was not a decision maker but needed to get permission from his boss. He was furious. I immediately apologized and tried to explain that what I really meant was accelerated – that things were speeding up. Everyone else showed understanding except for him.

The event went really well, and my customer received fantastic evaluations from their customers, but the person who got angry probably hasn't forgiven me yet…

THAT'S *not* WHAT SHE MEANT

I was about to give a lecture over lunch for some 200 of my client's VIP customers. This was in my birth town and I decided to bring my youngest son. He was about six years old. I asked my mother, who had never seen me on stage, if she wanted to tag along and see her son perform, while keeping her grandson in hand during my lecture. She said *Yes* and off we went.

While I was speaking, a lunch was served. Mushroom soup, fresh baked bread and more. After the speech, people approached me to have a chat. It took an hour before we could leave for Mum's home. When she put the keys in the door she said *"Well, at least I got some soup."*

I was appalled. *"What do you mean at least you got some soup?? Didn't you just see me, your son, on stage for the first time? I have yet to hear a simple Thank-you. I am glad you enjoyed the food but was I that bad?"* I was furious.

"No, no, no" she said. *"That's not what I meant. It was great to see you. I was only thinking about your son. He didn't like the food and it is way past lunchtime. I need to fix him something right away. I'm sorry, that's all I meant."*

Reflect on this:

How can you be clear in a conversation, without sounding blunt?

How can you ensure that the recipient has understood you?

How can you ensure that you yourself have understood the other person?

IF YOU CAN'T EXPLAIN IT
ON THE BACK OF A NAPKIN
YOU PROBABLY HAVEN'T
UNDERSTOOD IT YOURSELF.

HAVE YOU MISUNDERSTOOD
ANYONE THE LAST WEEK?

IF YOU SAID NO, YOU JUST
MISUNDERSTOOD THE QUESTION.

4. EVERYONE *affects* EVERYONE

Are you familiar with the theory "6 degrees of separation"? It says that everyone knows everyone on the planet within six steps. For example: I do not know Lady Gaga. However, I have a friend who knows a producer who does know her. Only three steps! Could it be possible, then, that Lady Gaga affects my mood? And now yours (step four)?

If Lady Gaga is in a good mood when she talks to the producer, she affects him with ... 15% more joy. He then meets my friend and she'll get affected with 10% more joy, transmitted. Then she meets me, and I become 5% happier – thanks to Lady Gaga! Isn't that amazing?

We are influenced by people we haven't even met. This means that feelings and emotions are contagious. When you go to a meeting, you bring your children and their morning temper. You bring the bus driver and the other passengers. You bring your social media contacts with all the guilt, joy, anger and wonder that their posts evoke in you. The others at the meeting do the same. How easy is it to be fully present when all this is going on?

You're like a rock being dropped in the ocean.

The wave is your emotional influence. You can now choose to be a positive force or a negative one, and whether you want to be a grain of sand, a big rock or maybe an asteroid, changing the course of the planet…

EVERYTHING THAT HAPPENED *before* WE MET

*I*sat in the cabin on row five, on my way to Sweden after a speaking assignment. On the other side of the narrow aisle sat an older gentleman. When the plane landed and the seat belt light went out, we did what we always do. We got up to take down our jackets and bags from the overhead compartment.

There isn't much personal space in those situations. You rub against each other and still keep a polite tone. The older man chose a different path. He gave me a scolding that was filled with insults, threats and more. Without going into details, the message was about my stupid and completely ruthless behavior, getting up at the same time as him.

Didn't I see that he got up first?
*Didn't I see that his seat was three inches in front of mine, and that I should therefore have gotten the f** out of his way?*

I moved slightly backwards to give him more space. It didn't
help. He elbowed me in the side. Then he leaned back
sharply so I was about to fall straight into the arms of two
Norwegians who witnessed everything with wide eyes. Both
shook their heads and started laughing. I said something
like *"He must have had a bad day"*. It didn't exactly help.
I couldn't keep quiet but pointed out both his elbows and
excessive cursing. Then he started to lean back all his weight
on me. I took one small step towards the Norwegians, which
made him lose his balance. I can't remember seeing anyone
so furious. He started to twitch his hands and I thought that I
might, for the first time since childhood, end up in some kind
of fight. Not something I wanted. I looked at him and said,
"What is your goal right now?" He answered, *"To never see
your face again!"*

I tried to think of the wise words of my smart friends. Like
Jan who, when he meets aggressive, unpleasant people,
always chooses to believe the best about them anyway.
That it's not about him, but about something else.

And Lena who says we have no idea what people are carrying
with them when they meet us, and that we should therefore
be kind. What wise people they are. And how difficult it is to
act that way when exposed to other people's antagonism.

Reflect on this:

If you are irritated – why is that?
Could it be about something that
happened way back?

Are people happy when you
show up, or when you leave?

Who do you bring to your work
(mentally)? Who do you leave
outside the front door?

DO YOU WANT TO BE A BIG ROCK
OR A TINY GRAIN OF SAND ?

5. ALL COMMUNICATION

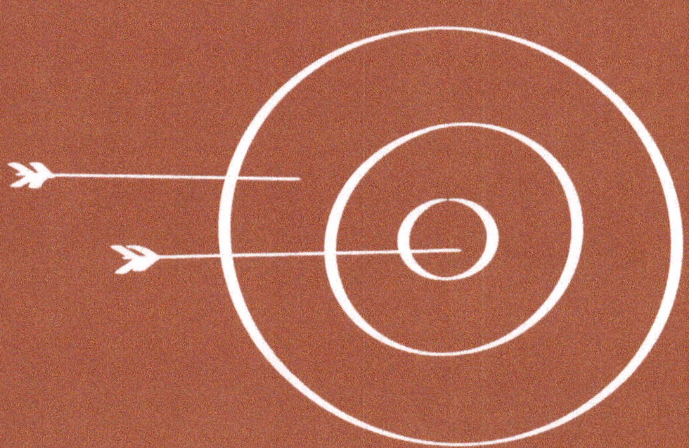

HAS AN *intention*

Who do you want to be? What do you want to achieve? How will you get there? Every time you communicate, you do so with an intention, or a goal. You want to feel good or make others feel good. You want to influence what others think and feel. You want to get a decision. You want to decide for yourself. All communication has an intention.

Sometimes the intention is hidden, even from yourself. You might yell at your loved ones, and not realize until the dust has settled that you were just hungry... Remember that "Everyone affects everyone". You might take out your anger on the wrong person. I know I have done that way too many times.

When you can share your goals and intentions so that they become clear, attractive, within your control and preferably challenging, then you will be able to cooperate easier and accomplish great deeds together with your colleagues.

If you can answer the question:
Then you have your values in place.

"Who do we want to be?"

If you can answer the question:
Then you know what result you want to reach.

"What should we achieve?"

If you can answer the question:
Then you know how to perform.

"How do we get there?"

A BOY, A CAP AND A *world champion*

I have a friend, Per, whose passion is motorcycles – everything about motorcycles, and the faster the better. This interest has caught on with his son Erik, who got his first motorcycle when he was about six years old. One beautiful summer day they were both at a track to watch the racing. Erik was in a good mood. Then Per saw Tony Rickardsson nearby!

For those of you who don't know: this man is a seven-times world champion at speedway! A living legend among motor enthusiasts. He went on, after his bike career, to win the Swedish version of Dance with The Stars, and that made him even more popular.

My friend Per saw Tony Rickardsson and the goal was set.
He would get his autograph for little Erik. He pushed his
way forward and reached Tony, took the red Ducati cap
from Erik's head and asked Tony for an autograph. Tony was
kindness personified. He smiled at Erik, got a pen, wrote his
autograph on the cap and then handed the cap to the boy.

Erik received it. He stared at the world champion with huge
eyes. Then he started to frown. He flung the cap onto the
dusty ground right in front of Tony's feet.
"Erik! What are you doing! " Said Per, who couldn't believe
what he was seeing.
"My cap is ruined!" Erik said.
"What?"

Erik said and stomped off. Behind him two surprised faces –
father's and superstar's – watched him march away.

Reflect on this:

Do you have clear goals at your workplace? So clear that you'll know if you succeed or not?

Do you have a common agreement of where you should be in a month, a year, five years?

How good are you at communicating goals between departments, so that you avoid conflicting goals and misunderstandings?

A MEETING WITHOUT A GOAL
IS NOT A MEETING.
IT'S A COFFEE BREAK!

6. BETTER TO *involve* THAN

TO INFORM

Many years ago, I attended a leadership program. Most things are forgotten by now, even though it was a really good course. However, some things stuck. One of them was a simple leadership model:

I > I > I
Involve > Inform > Implement

The thesis is:

- The ***more you involve***, the ***less you need to inform***. The implementation will be easier to obtain as well since people are more engaged in the process.
- If, on the other hand, you ***involve too little***, then you have to ***inform a lot***. People do not feel as engaged and so you risk never reaching the finish line.

We all want to feel involved and engaged. It gives us motivation. If we are motivated, we perform better (read Truth Number Two) and that leads to better results. Take your meetings as an example. What are the most boring meetings you go to? Correct answer: Information meetings. Someone puts you in a passive state and forces you to endure an hour or two of dry material, sometimes including plans/schedules/protocols for changes – new goals, new methods, new jobs for people to do.

Funnily enough, managers in that scenario believe that everything is ready, and that it is simply a matter of implementing the changes after such a meeting. That's humor!

THEY ARE *involved...*

I coached a manager who had difficulty getting his team to act on decisions.

"They don't do what we agree upon. It's so frustrating! I don't know what to do." He said.

"My experience is that the more people are involved, the easier it is to get them to act. So, my question to you is: Are they involved?" I asked.

"Of course, they're involved," the coachee said.

"How do you involve them?" I said.

"Well, they are in the meeting, and I tell them what to do, and they nod and agree. But then nothing happens ... "

"Isn't that informing rather than involving?"

It got quiet for a while. *"So, you mean...So, I have to really involve them?"*

"You decide for yourself. Imagine being one of the participants and your boss is telling you what to do without giving you a say in how to do it. How would that feel? "

"Not so good."

"As I see it, not everyone can be part of the outcome goals but everyone can be involved in how they should be reached. That's what they are experts in. "

"Damn, you're right. They aren't involved. I have to redo those meetings completely. "

The best QUESTION!

Have you ever felt that many meetings and conversations repeat themselves? It is the same old question – *What's up?* – in different shapes and forms. We already know where the answers lie, so it's not really a question of caring or exploring or solving, but rather Do you see me? Because I see you!

Lately I've been trying something new. It wasn't a conscious strategy. Suddenly one day during a golf round with an old friend a different kind of question came to me. I looked at my friend and asked:

> *"What's important?"*

Instead of providing an automatic reply, he stopped and thought before answering: *"We've moved the office and I get stuck in traffic queues. Now it's important for me to find a way not to be stressed. It might affect my family and I don't want that."* I listened, asked more questions and we discussed different ways of changing perspectives. It was rewarding. Even with someone I've known for decades, a whole new opportunity – an opportunity to get to know him even better – had opened up. *What's important?* This simple question opens new doors. It creates a deeper relationship. Try it for yourself and see what happens.

Reflect on this:

How can you transform your
information meetings into
involving meetings?

How can you coach colleagues
so that they grow and develop –
without micromanaging them?

What are your favorite ways of
involving people?

INFORMATION MEETINGS
ARE LIKE TAKING A SLEEPING PILL...
OR MANY.

7. ANALOG COMMUNICATION

IS SUPERIOR TO *digital*

Can you really feel the energy of the participants in a webinar? How well can you read the mood of everyone in a telephone conference – compared to a physical, real-face-to-real-face meeting? What about when you watch a concert online compared to being in the same room as the artist. Can you get the same feeling? Nope, it's not possible. The experience is different!

We humans are wired to communicate in the analog, physical way, around a campfire, or by the coffee machine. All other communication is poorer, more difficult…worse. Period.

Okay, there are clear benefits to digital communication. You save time and money on trips you don't have to make. You reduce the climate impact. You can access experts who don't have time to travel long distances just to attend a short meeting.

This doesn't make the actual meeting better, but sometimes "good enough" is the best you can hope for.

What if you need to have a delicate conversation? What if you have complex issues to discuss? What if you are running a workshop? My advice: Use analog communication whenever it's possible.

> *To be fair: We don't have digital meetings instead of analog ones. We have digital meetings instead of no meetings at all.*

THE WEBINAR FROM *Hell*

*F*riday. 12:30, right after lunch. I tried to log in to the webinar I was due to run at 13.00. I wanted to be ready in good time. The webinar tool was new to me. A partner of mine involved in the project wanted us to use it. She would be the moderator while I was giving a lecture on presentation skills to a group of ten people.

The day before we had tested the tools and it hadn't gone at all well. I wanted to use my iPad but it wasn't supported by the tool. Since I had a desktop computer without a webcam at the time, I needed another way. Fortunately, we had an old laptop at home, with a webcam. That would have to do.

At 12:35 I realized that I couldn't log in on the laptop. I decided to restart the computer. I shouldn't have. A ton of updates plus a slow computer wasn't the best formula for a quick reboot. It took forever (i.e. 30 minutes). I felt my heart rate go up and asked my colleague to cover up for me until I was logged in.

13:05 the computer was up again. Now I "just" had to log in, and start PowerPoint. That took another five minutes.

13:10 I was finally entering my own meeting. The webinar tool turned out to have another problem. It couldn't handle having a PowerPoint slide up on the screen and me on the webcam at the same time. I quickly chose PowerPoint. (See Truth Number 17 to get an idea of how I feel about that tool.) I immediately forgot that nobody could see me and started waving one of my books in front of the camera, until I realized my mistake.

I was now hyper-stressed and tried to regain control. Just as I started to get into a flow, my phone rang loudly . Damn! I apologized for the fourth time and continued. Just a moment later, the cleaner came in with a noisy vacuum cleaner. Now I was about to give up.

13:59:58 I finished this sad event and was about to thank the participants for their incredible patience, when the system was shut down. It turned out that it has a timer and at exactly 14:00 it was over. Like a door slamming in their faces ...

> *Is this a good time to tell you that I have written a book on how to lead virtual meetings?*

Reflect on this:

What meetings and conversations are best handled in the physical space and which ones are OK to do in the digital space?

How do you think your remote colleagues feel being connected to a conference phone, while the rest of you sit in the same room whispering, laughing, drawing things on your whiteboard which they can't see?

Do you have any ideas what your colleagues spend time on while participating in a phone conference? (The answer: "Other stuff…")

TO LEAD A PHYSICAL MEETING IS HARD. TO LEAD A VIRTUAL MEETING IS MUCH HARDER.

PART 2

---

13 HANDS-ON PRINCIPLES

---

8. First IMPRESSIONS LAST

*I*magine your brain having a bodyguard that constantly monitors what is happening around you. If you meet someone for the first time, the bodyguard will immediately want to know:

If the bodyguard feels in the least threatened, then it will take immediate command. There is no room for logical thinking. It would take too long. Now it is fight or flight that matters.
If the bodyguard decides that the person is not a threat, it will relax (somewhat) and let other parts of the brain take over – doing relationship building, engaging in dialogue, and other rational stuff.

In psychology jargon, this is called the priming effect, but we know it as the FIRST IMPRESSION. It happens at lightning speed and is completely beyond our conscious control.

You have many first impressions in your workplace. New people come and go, and each time, your bodyguard makes a decision whether it is red or green light. Either way – red or green, OK or not OK, friend or foe – you don't like to change your mind about someone once you have 'decided'. If you have approved someone then that person must be good. If you feel uncomfortable then the person must be stupid, wrong, a nuisance. You will fight to maintain your impression. It takes time to change a first impression. First impressions last.

THE POWER OF *the second* IMPRESSION

During the late eighties, I was in the military service. We were a platoon of telegraph communication recruits – 47 young men from near and far who gathered in the navy for six months of basic training before serving on different ships.

There were Jonas and Michael, two rock fanatics who found each other immediately. There was Anders with his hat on the side of his head and Per who snuck away to get a nap when no one was looking. There were others whom I hardly noticed and others who radiated cool but whose names I have forgotten. And then there was Stephen! A rather bland person with a bent back and thick glasses and a fragile body that didn't know how to swim. I wrote him off right away!

It wasn't that I did anything deliberately malicious to this kid. I just set him aside, like the clothes on the hangers in the department store that don't look quite your thing. No further thought. I didn't give him a chance, but instead started hanging out with the cool guys.

Several months into our time together, this changed. I don't remember the details, but I do know it was after Michael taught me to play my first chords on a borrowed guitar. That got Stephen and me talking. It turned out he himself was a musician. I asked if I could borrow one of his songs to practice. He said Yes and gave me the lyrics and chords, and I made a half-hearted attempt. The result of my interpretation was not remarkable in itself. More importantly, it was the interaction that made me open the door to Stephen and made me see him – for real – for the first time.

And what a great guy he was! His humor was quiet, smart and incredibly witty. His kindness was far more than I deserved. His musical ear was much better than mine. I came to like Stephen!

Dear Stephen (whose real name is something else),
I don't know where you are because we haven't had
contact since we were deployed on different ships over
thirty years ago. But wherever you are, I want you to know
that you made a fantastic second impression on me, and
for that I am deeply grateful to you!

Reflect on this:

What can you do, in order to create the best possible first impression – every time?

What impressions will other people have of you, on social media for instance?

Have you ever changed your mind about someone? How did that feel? What can you learn from it?

IT TAKES TIME TO CHANGE A FIRST IMPRESSION.
DO IT RIGHT THE FIRST TIME INSTEAD.
LOOK. SMILE. SAY SOMETHING NICE.

9. IF I AM LIKE YOU,

I TEND TO
like you

*H*ave you ever felt left out? Invisible? Have your colleagues gone for lunch without asking you to join? Have you ever felt the opposite – that you have been welcomed into a new group, that you have been listened to and that you have found common denominators with a new acquaintance (maybe an old TV program you have both seen or an advertisement tune you both can hum)?

We all want to feel that we belong. We want to be part of the tribe. We like people who are like us. We trust them more. We call it chemistry, or say we are on the same wavelength.
If you were thrown out of the pack 20,000 years ago, it would be like a death sentence.

Therefore, the followers will imitate the leaders. They want to be liked and approved.

Technically speaking, you can do three things to adapt to people. You can customize:
- **What you say.** If you have a customer who says "stream-line" then use the same word.
- **Your pace.** If you talk to someone …thoughtful, slow your own pace.
- **How you look.** Both in your body language and the way you dress.

THE WORST CUSTOMER MEETING *ever!*

I was in a splendid mood, on my way to a second meeting with one of Sweden's biggest companies. At the first meeting I met an HR manager. We clicked right away. *"There's this one small matter, though"* he said. *"I'm retiring in two weeks. But I will introduce you to my successor."* So now it was time to meet the successor. A young guy who was

. . . . S L O O O W . . .

He was moving slowly. He spoke slowly. And I was unable to adapt. I chattered on. At first with enthusiasm. Then I got nervous, jumpy. It went sideways. My pace, my examples. All wrong. I failed.

Afterwards, I slapped my hand on my forehead, embarrassed by this juvenile mistake. I called him on the phone. *"Thank you for letting me see you today. I thought it was a really bad meeting. "* I said. *"Whaaaaaaat?"* he replied, saying that No, No everything was fine, and we would get in touch later.

He never called me. He didn't answer my calls either. It was totally my fault and the only good thing about this whole mess is that I can share it with you here in my little catalogue of formative reminiscences.

WHEN I
changed school

When I was eleven, we moved to a new suburb. At that time, changing to a new school just felt like fun. But soon I realized that I was clearly not one of them.

One day I made the mistake of wearing a pair of beige leather shoes that my kind grandmother had bought for me. Everyone else was in Adidas or Puma. When my class mates saw them, they screamed, "Hello Shoey!" after me. I just smiled – but inside it hurt. I decided to wear my ugly shoes every day until they got tired. It took two weeks. Then they found someone new to bully. At that point I threw my beige leather shoes in the trash and went back to the sneakers I had always warn before my granny's gift.

I know that this incident is small potatoes compared to what some of you or your friends have experienced. That's why I rarely include such private examples in my lectures. It would be an insult to those who have had a much tougher time. However, I am convinced that my experiences, along with other situations, have made me think a lot about the Us-and-Them mentality that exists in so many places, and that's why I raise the issue in my lectures on communication and job satisfaction.

Reflect on this:

How can you contribute to a more inclusive workplace?

How can you make new employees, customers or vendors feel welcome?

How can you get rid of the bad-mouthing trash talk that sometimes occurs between departments?

THE BIGGER US
THE SMALLER THEM

WHAT IF ALL PEOPLE THOUGHT:

"I AM OK
AND SO ARE YOU."

10. IT'S BETTER TO BE *interested*

THAN INTERESTING

So many studies come to the same conclusion:

If you are a manager or team-mate and (perhaps because you are under stress) you answer before your colleagues have asked the whole question, they will get annoyed, hurt and irritated. I myself have been on both ends of such clumsy, painful conversations. They provide no engagement at all.

The opposite is also true. When you converse with someone who is curious, who asks follow-up questions and who is genuinely interested, the motivation and desire to perform skyrocket.

This is directly linked to the superpower of Empathy (remember the beginning of the book?). Empathy, in turn, creates trust, and trust is one of the finest words we have. Showing interest is how you get loyal and motivated employees and colleagues. It's when a good salesperson displays interest that they win the business, not at the end of the process.

A bonus: If you are interested instead of interesting – you become interesting! It is a paradox. How many people are really interested in you? Not many, it turns out. Most are so occupied with themselves. Those who are interested are therefore a special set of people, standing out in the crowd.

"THANKS FOR A GREAT
discussion!"

A few years ago, I moderated a sales conference for a building company. In the evening there was a dinner with an award ceremonty which I was to lead.

I found an empty spot at the dinner table and looked around. To my left sat a man who can best be described as… gray. His clothes were gray, his hair was gray, his skin was gray. He had hardly any charisma at all. This was my first impression of him. I grabbed myself by the scruff of the neck and deliberately went for a curious mindset.

I asked what he was doing outside of work. He blossomed! With great enthusiasm, he talked about his passion for helping young people who have had a tough time at home for this or that reason. He was no longer gray, he was radiating all the colors of the rainbow. Time flew by. It was a joy to listen to him. After 45 minutes it was time for the awards ceremony. I got up from my chair and excused myself. He also got up, took my hand and shook it vigorously, saying *"Thanks for a good discussion!"*

That talk had many ingredients but there was no discussion whatsoever. Not that it mattered. I learned my lesson and I'm happy about the way I became interested instead of interesting.

WHAT'S THE DIFFERENCE BETWEEN *Hearing* AND *Listening?*

When one of my sons was six years old, I asked him: *"Can you tell me the difference between hearing and listening?*

He looked at me with a raised eyebrow and replied:

"You're the consultant. You should know that."

"Well yes, but I'm interested in your opinion," I said.

"Okay Dad, pay attention," he said. *"To hear is simply not being deaf. But to listen is when you really try to understand what the other person is saying, Dad, and not only what they're saying but also what they really mean. "*

I looked at the boy for three seconds in silence. Then I said, in my most commanding voice:

"Welcome to the company, my son!"

Reflect on this:

What kind of climate do you have at work?
Open and trustworthy or closed and
suspicious?

What kind of listening do you have?
Do you listen with the intent to understand,
or to answer?

Do you ask mostly closed questions
(with answers like *Yes, No, Maybe*)
or open questions (that start with *What,
Who, How, Why, Which, When, Where*)?
Or do you have problems asking questions
at all?

STRANGE...
YOU LEARN MORE IF YOU LISTEN
INSTEAD OF TALKING.
WHAT HAVE YOU LEARNT TODAY?

THE LONGER THE QUESTION

THE SHORTER THE ANSWER

11. WORDS *matter!*

ords can strengthen people or hurt them. Words build or destroy. Words can make you feel alive or numb, smart or dumb.

There are weak words and strong words. If you are a manager: Don't say Them or They. Those are weak words. Say Me, We and You. These are strong words.

Use fewer, better words. Imagine that you are invited to two meetings that will occur at the same time. You ought to be at both, but that will obviously not happen. Then you read the invitations:

You colleague Joel writes:
"I thought we could have a little meeting, where we can chat about our new product and maybe think about if there is any new target group that might be interested in trying it out, so let's meet for a while. I have booked two hours and of course there will be coffee and muffins, I hope you will come, it would be nice, but you don't have to, there is so much to do, I will understand…"

Johanna says:
"We have 90 minutes. The goal is for us to list five prioritized market segments for our upcoming product. We will appoint one responsible per segment and, at the next meeting, have a draft of a marketing plan. See you at 13:15. "

Which meeting will you attend? Joel's or Johanna's?

ONE SENTENCE, AND HE
quit his job

I was in Silicon Valley for some training in the late 90's. We were around a dozen people attending classes and having team-building activities. At one point we visited a redwood forest. These magnificent trees can be 50 meters high. Between two of the trees, there were ten horizontal beams spaced about 1.5 meters apart. The task was to try to climb this giant ladder all the way up. I signed up as a volunteer.

While I was strapping on my harness a colleague, Jan, looked at me worriedly.

"Do you dare to do that?" he asked. "Why of course, if I don't stretch my comfort zone, it will shrink."

I replied, thinking of it no more. Instead, I climbed nine beams before falling.

Two years later I met Jan's wife, who worked at the same company. *"How is Jan? I haven't seen him since we were in the US,"* I asked. *"You haven't heard? When he came home, he went straight to his boss and resigned. He said that you mentioned something about stretching your comfort zone. Something resonated within him. He's at a start-up company now. "*…

KEEP YOUR *word*

I was 14 years old and I was struggling in my football (soccer) club IFK Gothenburg. The growing pains in my knees and heels were slowing me down. The club physician said I needed a change of shoes, but I knew that my family couldn't afford it, so I kept them, and suffered. Soon I got benched.

"Your style works better on grass," my coach said, giving me hope. (Most games at that time were played on gravel.) I kept fighting and then, after a few months, the time came for a game on proper grass. Finally! In the dressing room the team got instructions from the coach, and I was told that I would be a substitute. Again. I was disappointed but sure I would get a chance to play. I was so pumped up!

The first half came and went. My friend Thomas and I sat by the side. The second half began. A quarter-hour later, the coach finally turned to us.
"Thomas, warm up. You're going in," said the coach. And so he did. The game continued. The coach made no more changes...

A month later I changed club, and I had some good years. The growing pain went away, and I got back on the field again. I don't think I have forgiven the coach for what he did. His words gave me hope at first and then a disappointment that really hurt my feelings.

Reflect on this:

Do you have a generous, positive atmosphere at work, and does it show in how you talk to each other?

What do you do if a colleague is mean to someone?

Have you ever had someone express real faith in you and your potential? What happened with you then?

"A PICTURE CAN GENERATE
A THOUSAND WORDS.
BUT A WORD CAN GENERATE
A THOUSAND PICTURES."
— MIA LILJEBERG

WHAT IF IT'S TRUE
THAT YOU GET HALF OF
ALL PRAISE IN YOUR LIFETIME...

...BEFORE YOU TURN THREE.

TALK ABOUT ROOM FOR IMPROVEMENT!

12. KEEP IT *simple* NOT STUPID

The maturation of your communication is a three-step process.

First, you use simple communication – because you don't know any better. For instance, you come to a new workplace, perhaps a new industry, and you haven't learned the jargon yet.

Eventually you learn, and now you are at step two: You complicate things. You throw around acronyms, industry jargon and internal lingo.

Most people stay on stage two…

But there are those who get to step three. They communicate in clear and concrete language. They communicate knowledge and competence, but they keep it simple. They simplify (like Obama) without dumbing it down (like the one who came after).

It is much easier to be complicated than to be simple. It takes time and effort to use clear, concrete language, but it also becomes much easier for the recipient to understand what you are saying, so it's worth it.

Think about the butterfly metaphor. First you are a caterpillar. Then you're in a cocoon. Don't stay in the cocoon. Become a butterfly!

"AHA, YOU'RE A *moderate leader.*"

When one of my sons was seven, he asked me: *"Dad, what do you work with? What kind of job do you have?"*

I gave it a few seconds' thought, and then said:
"I'm like Lisbeth, your teacher, though I have adult students… And I write books, too."
"I know," he said. *"Boring books. No pictures at all. "*
"True, I'll fix that in my future books. But you know when we watch Idol on TV. I am like a program leader. Only my guests won't sing, they are talking."
"Aha," he said. *"You're a talk-leader."*
What a good expression, right? I should have said Yes, but instead I went the smart-ass way.
"Yes, my son, but it's called a moderator."
He looked at me and said *"Okay, so you are a moderate leader…"*

> *Actually, my son was probably more correct than I normally care to admit!*

DON'T UNDERESTIMATE PEOPLE'S *intelligence,* BUT DON'T OVERESTIMATE THEIR *knowledge*

*C*ustomers don't want to feel stupid, but it is so easy for that to happen if the supplier uses phrases that have no meaning outside the supplier's internal world. It can be perceived as exclusion, which is the opposite of what the customer wants. This is especially evident when I train product specialists, technical support staff and other engineers before working in a booth at a trade show and communicating with visitors. The same goes for tech specialists making presentations to people with only a general level of knowledge.

I have noticed how buzzwords have infected people. A telecom company I work with changes their favorite words at least every year. One year it's the word *"mitigate"* and the next it's all about *"monetize."* Then they go for *"agile"*…and so it goes on.

I usually ask, *"What is it that you really want to say?"* It's so interesting to hear their answers because it is then that they say the most concrete things. *"What I really want to say is that we adapt along the way instead of being so rigid"* (Agile). or *"We want to help our clients make money"* (Monetize). So then I ask, *"Why don't you say that?"*

Reflect on this:

What acronyms and abbreviations do you throw around in your workplace? Do you use internal lingo to external people, and other expressions that few people get?

If you're asked what you do for a living; what would you say?

Have you ever tried 'Bullshit Bingo' (more politely named 'Buzzword Bingo')? As you enter the conference room, the organizer hands you a bingo card – typically a six-square grid. Instead of a random half-dozen of the numbers between 1 and 90 (classic parlor game Bingo)…your boxes contain acronyms (ROI, NDA), current in-house label-words (agile, monetize), and corporate clichés (big picture, leverage). As the various speakers deliver their stuff, you keep track – ticking each of your squares as its buzzword is delivered. Got all six? You've won!

The polite old way of claiming the prize (and getting a laugh from the audience and a gasp of horror from the speaker) is to cry out "BINGO!" Less politely, you might scream "BULLSHIT!"

IT'S SO MUCH EASIER TO BE COMPLICATED THAN TO BE SIMPLE.

13. EXPLAIN *the value*

NOT THE FEATURES

I'm guessing that you are a manager, a salesperson, a customer service type or an office employee with some other function. Let's say you want others to buy your product, your service, your proposal, your bright idea. Then you should know that all people tune in to the same radio channel: WII FM. (Do you remember from the beginning of the book?) OK, an acronym, meaning What's In It For Me? What does it give me the listener? What does that mean for us the wider audience?

If you can answer this unspoken question, then you have ex-plained the value – the benefit of your idea, product or service. Then it becomes attractive. Then it feels good. Then they can make decisions. If not, then you've probably gone into…the feature-trap.

Go into any electronics store. Let the counter staff know that you are interested in a new computer, TV, phone or whatever. Now notice how they will talk only about features like gigahertz, gigabytes, megapixels or megabits per second. Boring! No-one buys hertz, bytes, pixels or bits…

Let's assume that one billion drills are sold each year in in the world. Nobody wants a drill! What do they want? A hole. Why? They want a happy home with a beautiful painting, a nice tidy bookshelf or a smart welcoming table.

> *Talk value and people will be interested. Talk features and most people switch off or get confused. Your choice.*

THE *dumbest* ADVICE

I remember listening to another sales coach and his lesson on how to "catch" a customer. He said two things that made me react in different ways. First, he said: *"You always sell the future. You might say: With this product you'll be able to do A."*

I thought this made sense. What you buy today is supposed to give you a reward later. But then he went on and gave the dumbest advice I have heard in this business:
"If the customer then says: 'Not interested'– then you continue with B, C, D and so on. In the end, the customer will say: 'Well THAT is interesting to us.' Now you've got them!"

My reaction? "What a waste of time!"

If you follow his advice, you make two mistakes at the same time:
1. You show that you haven't listened (see Truth Number 10, about being interested instead of interesting)
2. You have made your offering expensive, because the customer now realizes that they have to pay for some features that they are not interested in.

Don't follow that sales coach's stupid advice. Find out what is important to the customer and why. Then focus on explaining the value of your solution according to what the customer has told you.

BUT IT'S A
good price!!

I was in Lisbon on vacation one summer. We were in this big square and I was waiting for my girlfriend to come out of a restaurant. A young man came walking towards me. He wore dirty clothes and his hair hadn't seen a comb for quite a while, I would guess. He smiled at me and raised his eyebrows.

"Hashish?" he said.

"No thanks."

"It's a good price."

"I am not interested."

Then he got upset.

"BUT IT'S A GOOD PRICE!!"

I didn't know how to respond to that. He couldn't grasp that the price of his product was completely irrelevant for me. Luckily, my girlfriend saved me by coming out from the restaurant, and we quickly left the square.

Reflect on this:

How do you rate your ability to find out what's important and why, when talking with colleagues or customers?

Do you slip into the feature-trap when selling a product, service or idea, explaining bits and bytes, delivery times and prices…instead of the value it brings?

Do you pause for a moment after you've explained the value? Or do you nervously ramble on?

TO SERVE IS TO HELP CLIENTS AND
COLLEAGUES WITH WHAT THEY NEED.
NOT WITH WHAT YOU WANT.
AND IT HAS NOTHING TO DO WITH TENNIS...

14. *The beginning* AND *the end*

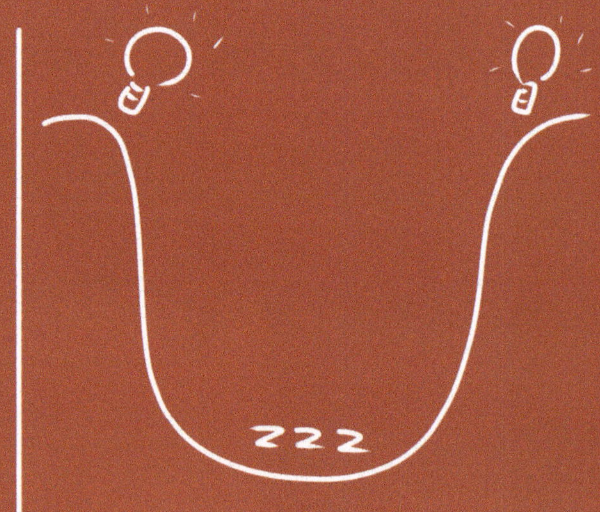

ARE MOST IMPORTANT

Read the following words aloud, one by one:
Phone, Music, Meetings, Tennis, Leader, Lemon, Slow, Spin, Loose, Michael Jackson,Spirit, Possible, Find, Optimize, Flow, Rent, Ketchup, Blood, Red, End

Now bring out a paper and pen. Put this book aside and write every word you remember. No cheating!

…Welcome back. Chances are, you have written down the first words and the last words, with a few exceptions. In the middle you can hardly remember anything. But there is one item that most people remember in addition to those at the beginning and the end. Can you guess? Yes, it's Michael Jackson!

Are you presenting things to your colleagues or customers? Make sure that what you say and do in the beginning and at the end are well practiced, that you are to the point and clear, and that you are as concrete as you can be.

We humans remember these parts the most.

And then you add some of the coming success factors 15 and 16 as well…

IT SOUNDED LIKE A *good idea* BUT...

Sometimes people do strange things to get attention. Sure enough, they get attention, but in the wrong way. Here are two conversations I've had with friends, both of whom came away with fresh insights:

"I remember one of my teachers at the university. On the first lesson in the auditorium, he came in and started the whole thing by dropping all his papers on the floor. It turned out to be a thing he did with every new class to get attention. And he really succeeded. I still remember it today. " "Yeah, but do you remember any of what he said during that lesson?"

"Um ... nah ..."

"I was at a lecture and the woman speaking initially told us that she was going to show us a picture of herself naked. The last thing she screened was a picture of herself as a baby. Everyone laughed. I remember it as if it were yesterday. "
"Yeah, but do you remember any of her messages during the lecture?"

"Um ... nah ..."

DO IT *James Bond* STYLE

I met a playwriter who explained how each event, lecture, film or stage drama was structured in much the same way – a three-step process. He used James Bond as an example.

Act 1: The first chase.
Bond pursues someone on land, at sea, by car, on a train, in a helicopter or just running and jumping.
This corresponds to an eye-opening introduction. Here you get people to understand why they should pay attention to you.

Act 2: Now the story begins.
You find out who the villain is and who the good guys are. Unexpected events and people challenge Bond in different ways. Events build up.
This corresponds to the main body of your presentation/ speech/lecture. This is the hardest part if you don't have any Michael Jacksons to lift the audience's interest.

Act 3: Everything is at its peak.
Will Bond survive? YES! He succeeds. The villain dies in an explosion. Everyone sighs with relief. The world is saved. Bond takes a Russian spy to bed.
This is your ending. Here you tie things together so that the message is repeated one last time (Bond is a brave hero and irresistible to women).

Reflect on this:

How do you start a meeting or presentation? Are you showing an unbearably boring agenda, or do you have a better ritual?

How do you end the meeting or presentation? Do you apologize and say "Oops, I'm late for the next meeting! See you in a week ", or do you summarize the most important points and next steps?

What do you do in the middle of the presentation so that people remember? Do you show yet another 20 slides or do you share relevant examples and stories and ask engaging questions?

EVERY BEGINNING HAS AN END.
EVERY END, A BEGINNING.

15. THREE IS THE

magic NUMBER

How many gifts did the wise men bring Jesus when he was born? How many companions did Dorothy have when she traveled through Oz? How many wishes did the magic fish give the fisherman?

How many bears did Goldilocks meet when she woke up in their home? How many pigs messed with the big bad wolf? How many nephews does Donald Duck have?

We remember things in threes! If you look around you will find that this figure is magical. Everywhere we meet it. Fill in:
Sex and drugs and ___*
Hope, Faith and _____*
Blood, Sweat and _____* This one comes from Winston Churchill who actually gave a list of four in his speech. The fourth, Toil, is remembered by no one. A blemish on the record of an otherwise brilliant communicator.

Use your own triads if you want people to remember what you say. For example, when you want to sell an idea, you give three arguments. One for credibility (Ethos), one for reason (Logos) and one for feeling (Pathos). Enjoy the wonderful feeling of being able to communicate memorably.

(* The missing words above are: Rock'n'roll; Love [or Charity – depending on which version of the Bible you grew up with]; Tears.)

11 BONUS *tips* TO MAKE PEOPLE REMEMBER WHAT YOU *said*

1. Use alliterations

Word starting with the same sound, like Back to Basics, or Veni, Vidi, Vici. It creates a nice rhythm.

2. Ask probing questions

"Do you remember when ... What did you learn from that?" Questions make people dig for answers and that helps the stuff stick in the memory.

3. Use polarities and contrasts

This stays in the memory ... we're a binary creature. Is it black or white, thick or narrow, hard or soft?

4. Repeat

Memory improves as the message is repeated. We also recognize the repetition as deliberate. This means that if you repeat something, people will remember it better. Got it?

5. Plant a trigger

If you say that values are like a filter and at the same time
display a coffee filter, then people will associate the coffee and
the filter with values each time they make themselves a cup.

6. Tell stories

More about that in Truth Number 16.

7. Reinforce the content with gestures

See more in Truth Number 18.

8. Be relevant

What is relevant is interesting. What is interesting we remember.

9. Be emotional

It sparks the recipients' brains and hearts and makes them
remember better.

10. Use metaphors and parables

A marvelous shortcut between your brain and theirs.

11. Create a one-liner

Like "You had me at Hello." Something that people can reuse
and repeat (back to tips number 4).

Reflect on this:

How can you boost your messages by using the power of 3?

How do you yourself remember content?

Try some of the other techniques. How did it go? How can you improve even more?

"ONE, TWO, THREE, ...MANY"
– MY SON WHEN HE WAS THREE

THE THREE SUPERPOWERS
OF COMMUNICATION

ENERGY

EMPATHY

CLARITY

16. STORYTELLING
rules!

Do you remember what happened to me in Lisbon?
Do you remember Jan asking how I dared to climb those high trees? Do you remember the fruit baskets and the business class tickets?

Since we first developed a spoken language, we have used stories to describe what is important to us, to carry on traditions and to create a community. We have been sitting around campfires, in caves and in tents. We have passed on our ancestors' knowledge – and rules for life – through stories. Throughout this book, I have shared memories and examples in order for you to remember better.

We buy the story more than the product we are interested in. We buy the story more than the company where we are seeking a job. We buy the story more than the leader's job-title. Storytelling rules!

If you want to bypass the brain's intellectual doorman (who can only review the facts), then share a story. The gatekeeper will open the door and point to the limbic system where the emotions sit and say: "Our CEO sits there. She might understand what you're talking about. I can't judge it. "

WHEN *an idol* CAME TO TOWN

When I found out that Glenn Stromberg would come to a town close to where I lived, giving a lecture about his life as a football player, I dropped everything and drove to the venue. 200 people had gathered in a hotel restaurant where he would speak.

On the way there, I remembered playing for the same team he did, IFK Gothenburg, but I was a young boy of 14 and he was in the A-team. He and the team won the UEFA Cup in 1982 (now called Europa league). I was right there on the side lines cheering at the quarter final, the semi-final and the final. Glenn was a young player who would continue his career as a professional in Portugal and Italy.

I saw Glenn as soon as I arrived and I was a bit star-struck. After a nervous attempt to converse with him, I sat down.

Glenn was presented and took over. For two hours he talked without any breaks. Everything was about memories and anecdotes. We were hypnotized.

From a pure presentation skills perspective, there were opportunities for improvement. But it didn't matter at all. We were on the field with him. We could feel the soft grass and the hard tackles. We were beside him when he sought a penalty and fell. We enjoyed it, laughing and applauding. It was a delight. Thank you, Glenn, for the gift you gave!

"I DON'T REMEMBER A WORD YOU SAID, BUT YOU WERE *awesome!*"

Working in a telecom company outside Stockholm, I was on a sidewalk on my way to a galleria for some lunch. On the other side of the street I noticed a man staring at me. With determined steps, he crossed the street and came straight towards me. Hesitantly, I stopped and waited for him. When he was really close, he said, *"It's you! It's you! "*

"Yes," I said. *"It's me. But who are you?"*

"I'm your colleague and I attended your launch event in Boca Raton (USA). You were on stage. Do you remember?"

I did remember, even though some years had passed. It's not often you get standing ovations. *"Well, yes I remember. You were there?"*

"I was. And I just have to say, you were AWESOME! "

I grew inches. *"Thank you."* I said…humbly.

"I don't remember a word you said, but you were AWESOME!" He continued. *"Ah, yeah … Yeah thanks again."* I went my way, full of doubt about myself. What had gone wrong?

In retrospect, I can admit that I had made a really good presentation from a non-verbal perspective. But there were zero memory hooks. No story, no concrete examples. Nothing. Yakety yak!

Reflect on this:

When you present, is it all facts, Excel and statistics?

How can you, with simple examples, make your messages more memorable?

How can you help the recipient to create pictures, sounds, feelings etc. with the help of stories?

FACTS WITHOUT A STORY ARE BORING. STORIES WITHOUT FACTS ARE JUST ENTERTAINMENT. BUT A STORY WITH FACTS ARE PURE MAGIC!

17. POWERPOINT SUCKS! –

or does it?

*F*ew things in the workplace can suck the life energy out of people more than bad managers, bad meetings and bad PowerPoint slides. Combine these three and you get an organization in crisis!

So many awful information meetings are out there. Pure torture! A marathon of unbearable slides full of bullet points, small fonts, illegible charts and long sentences that the speaker either reads out loud or says *"I know it's hard to read, but what this slide says is ..."* To complete the suffering, they decorate the crap with a stupid flower, handshake or staircase. Useless!

Stop it right now! Just because you have had to endure those poorly prepared speakers and their rotten slides, that doesn't mean you have to make everyone else go through the same pain. Or are you one of those who thinks it's wise to 'pay it forward' – bad experiences as well as favors and good turns! That doesn't create engagement. It doesn't create motivation. Just stop!

PowerPoint is like alcohol, drugs and tobacco.

You may get high on your addiction, but everyone else will suffer.

Because it's the abuse I'm talking about. It is not the tool's fault. It's yours!

IT TOOK *ten years*

When I left my employment in 2006 to start my own company, I was so allergic to PowerPoint that I refused to use the tool for ten years. Except once, in 2011, when the customer told me I had to. I explained that I didn't use slides, and that I wanted a flipchart instead.

So, I drew an S-shaped curve on an iPad, converted it to a picture and pasted it on a slide. Then I talked about successful customer meetings for twenty minutes, with this single image in the background. It was a relevant picture; no decoration, and the lecture went well.

A few years back, I started using PowerPoint again. The pictures you see in this book are my illustrations. And that's what my slides look like today. I pair the headings you see in the chapters with the pictures. That's all. A short text and a relevant picture make people remember better. Now it's fun to use PowerPoint again, although I can't be as flexible as I want. I still go analog when I can with a flipchart, or just storytelling.

A PICTURE. *A* WORD. *A* NUMBER

A global company brought me in for preparations and training before going to a gigantic trade show. 200 people from the company would work in a 6,000-square-meter booth. The company wanted all those people to know more about the different offerings at the fair, what product areas were represented, what the most important messages were for each business area and what important launches they would promote. The risk was obvious that Death by PowerPoint would occur.

I came up with an idea and pitched it at the person responsible for the booth staff. *"How about forcing the presenters to have only three slides each? One picture. One word. And one number. This will make them focus. It will also help their colleagues remember."* The idea was approved with nervous enthusiasm.

Rarely have I seen so many interested employees in this company during presentations. No phones were picked up. Everyone really listened. It was so cool. The first few performances, anyway…

Then four more people went up to present. They had never "got the memo" and had the typical corporate slides. I looked around in the room. Immediately people started to fiddle around with their phones, whisper to each other or simply doze off…

Reflect on this:

Do you use slides so that you will remember what to say, or to help the audience?

If the participants expect handouts, do you make two versions? One to read when you're not around, and one simpler for when you present?

Are you using a font size so small that it's hard to read? Why on earth…?

TO SHOW YOUR SPEAKER NOTES ON THE SLIDE
TO THE PARTICIPANTS IN A MEETING
IS LIKE SHOWING YOUR USED TOILET PAPER
TO ALL GUESTS AT THE RESTAURANT.

18. YOUR BODY SPEAKS *louder* THAN WORDS

*L*ong before we invented the spoken word, we had body language. When people gesture, those around will detect intentions. A raised eyebrow. A sneering lip. A glance over the shoulder. Smiling eyes. Hands raised towards the sky. A foot that stomps. Everything sends signals that we interpret. Sometimes we are right. Sometimes we are dead wrong.

Did you know that the difference between looking arrogant or normal, is just one inch – 2.54 cm? Try talking to someone and then, halfway in, raise your nose an inch…

If you stare at someone for too long, you send signals of either domination or lust. Non-verbally, that means you want either to fight or to make babies.

If you grip your hands in front of you ('washing your hands'), you send signals of nervousness and/or excitement. The recipients will perceive it, and they will find it harder to focus on what you say than on what you do. Body language always wins!

> *Use your body to reinforce your message,*
> *to show that you are listening, to help colleagues*
> *feel safe or encouraged.*

"HOW YA *doin'*?"

I was holding presentation skills training and had just introduced body language, and how long we should have eye contact with someone.

"Three seconds is just right. If you look away too quickly you will be perceived as nervous, and you won't be credible. But if you are "psycho-staring" at someone for too long, you are either aggressive or extremely flirtatious. I guess you don't want the audience at the event to feel either of those. "

One of the participants started smiling and she said *"Aha!"* *"What?"* I wondered. *"Do tell!"*
"Well," she began. *"I was to give a presentation recently. It was on a large stage, one where you look down at the audience. There were quite a few people there and I was a bit nervous. I decided to take a look at a nice-looking guy to the left. At first, he was neutral. After a while he looked puzzled, like he was trying to figure something out. But then he leaned his head a little and gave me a smile, like Joey in the 'Friends' series, just before Joey says "How ya doin?"*

She laughed. *"I had no idea I was flirting with him, but now I realize it."*

QUICK *tips*

Hands in your pockets when presenting may be perceived as nonchalant – uncaring, apathetic.

Arms that are locked at the elbow limit your range of gestures, so you get repetitive.

If you want to reinforce the message you should move while you talk and then "freeze" the movement when you are silent. That brings clarity (and forces you to pause).

If you make a wide gesture, don't pull your arm back towards the body as if a rubber band has twanged. Instead, keep the arm outstretched for a few seconds.

When you greet people, extend both arms in a welcoming gesture. Hold the gesture.

If you are saying something less important, meriting no rein-forcement, let your arms hang loose by your sides.

Feel free to walk around, but with some purpose. Don't wander aimlessly.

If your palms point upwards, then you are inclusive and curious. If they point downwards, you are confident – and uninterested in the opinions of others. Use these gestures wisely.

Reflect on this:

What gestures can you use to strengthen your messages and bring clarity?

Film yourself the next time you present. What was good? What can be better?

Have you noticed how some people radiate authority or high status without saying a word? How can that be?

Bonus: When it comes to how you look, you can augment the symbolic language with your clothes, hair style, jewelry, tattoos and more. What signals do you send with your symbolic language? How do you perceive other people based on that?

YOUR BODY SCREAMS SO LOUD,
I CAN'T HEAR WHAT YOU SAY...

THE DIFFERENCE BETWEEN
LOOKING ARROGANT OR NORMAL
IS ONLY ONE INCH.

LIFT YOUR NOSE ONE INCH
THE NEXT TIME YOU TALK TO SOMEONE.
FEEL THE DIFFERENCE!

19. YOUR VOICE *strengthens* OR *sedates*

*I*magine walking in a forest. Everything is calm and quiet. The only things you hear are the birds chirping and a gentle breeze. You come down to a stream where the water is moving slowly away from you.

Then you hear a twig being broken. All your attention goes toward that sound – immediately!

- Is there a creature that wants you for dinner?
- Or a creature that you might eat?
- Is there someone who wants to harm you?
- Or is there someone you can ... mix your DNA with to create new little people?

Your brain has a built-in radar that constantly searches for the unexpected. If everything seems quiet, then your thoughts start to wander. "What will you do later today? Did you lock the door when you left home? Aren't you a bit hungry? Have you received any likes on your latest LinkedIn post? "

Your colleagues' brains work exactly the same way. Everything monotonous is harmless, boring and filtered away. You have to be incredibly relevant or considered a guru in your industry for someone to be able to listen to you drone monotonously at the same pace and volume all the time. That way of speaking is just great for bedtime stories where you actually want your kids to fall asleep, but…

Don't be the gentle wind. Don't be the slow stream. Be the twig!

WHAT ELSE *can* YOU DO?

*I*f you want to keep your colleagues interested and focused on what you're delivering, a dynamic voice is one of your best tools. Here's a number of ways to put color in your voice.

Vary your pitch. When your pitch goes down at the end of the sentence, you state a fact or an opinion. When your voice goes up at the end of the sentence you ask a question.

Vary your pace. By slowing down in some parts and speeding up in others, you create both curiosity and interest.

Vary your volume. Increase it when you want to show strong emotions. But if you are a boss, remember that you are sending on a "high volume" anyway. Sometimes, lowering your volume is even better when you want to make a point.

Emphasize in the right places – pitch and/or volume. Then people will understand that this bit is really important.

Pause – more often than you think. If you pause before something important you draw people in to you. If you pause afterwards, you create room for reflection.

Remove all err.. and hmm.. sounds. They are annoying! Replace them with ... silence.

THE VOICE *champions* OF THE WORLD

There are many amazing leaders and inspiring people out there, so to pick the best is virtually impossible. Yet I will give it a try and highlight three:

Winston Churchill. It wasn't only his words that sparked action, but also his emphasis and repetition of certain phrases (eg "We shall fight…We shall fight…We shall never surrender") His speeches on the radio during the war are perhaps the most important ones in modern times.

Greta Thunberg. If you don't know who she is, you have been living under a rock the last year or so. Still, her voice is not her greatest asset, it's her laser-sharp messages, just like with Churchill. But her quiet, steady voice is like an inevitable avalanche. There is no escape, no room to hide. If you are a leader who doesn't care for the next generation, she will call you out.

Barack Obama. Google 'Hope Obama' on YouTube. You'll get a music video from 2008 where you'll hear that he has a rhythm that musicians can use to create a song. Unbelievably cool!

Reflect on this:

Is there a difference in your voice
when you stand up in front of
people, compared to sitting down
at a conference table?

How can you use your voice to
create comfort or discomfort, safety
or fear, curiosity or certainty?

Do you use non-words like hmm..
and err.. when you speak? Can you
replace them with pauses?

"DID YOU BUY MILK TODAY?"
"WELL SOMEBODY NEEDED TO."

"DID YOU BUY MILK TODAY?"
"NO I STOLE IT."

"DID YOU BUY MILK TODAY?"
"YES, SHOULD I HAVE BOUGHT
WINE OR WHAT?"

"DID YOU BUY MILK TODAY?"
"I FORGOT TO BUY IT
YESTERDAY SO..."

20. BRAVE *people*

WIN BIG

*I*f you are a salesperson, your job is to sell. If you don't have the courage to get a decision from the customer, you'll be miserable, and you won't keep your job.

Isn't it true that you want your colleagues to like your idea of a new espresso machine? Or you want your boss to appreciate the merits of a new supplier? Or you want the beautiful person you met at yoga class to come with you on a date?

It's just at the crucial moment that many people chicken out. Despite sensing a positive interest, they dread failure. So they don't push for a commitment. Make or break? That's too scary!
"What if it I get a No? Then I am worthless!"
No, you are not.

Be brave. Be bold. Be just a bit pushy. If your proposal is a good proposal, then it's smart to do whatever you can to get it accepted.

BIG DECISIONS TAKE
less time

I lived in Gothenburg, the second biggest city in Sweden. She was from a small village from the south of Sweden and now lived in the capital: Stockholm. *"I think we should move in together,"* I said. *"I agree,"* she said.

I showed her everything beautiful in Gothenburg. The parks, the old town, the harbor, that one summer day when it was sunny... Then we moved to Stockholm.

Nine years later I said *"Our firstborn son is starting school this fall. It's time to move."* *"I agree,"* she said. *"To my hometown."* *"Okay, get a job,"* I said. *"I'll start my own company"*

She flew down and looked at a house. *"It has potential,"* she said on the phone. *"We buy it!"* I said. *"Don't you want to see it?"* She said. *"It's not necessary. I trust you. "* I said.

Once there, I called a car dealer. *"Do you have an environmental-friendly Volvo to sell?"* I said. *"I have one that you can buy,"* said the seller. *"I'll take it,"* I said.

Then I went to buy a jacket. I posed for 45 minutes in front of the store's mirror. *"Do you really think it fits me well?"* I asked, for the fifth time. *"Yes,"* said the seller, bored. *"I have to think about it,"* I said and walked out. I bought the jacket a whole week later. Strange how difficult it can be sometimes...

Three DECISION STYLES

*I*magine three managers with different decision styles. How can you help them make a timely decision, given that they are interested? Here are some tips:

The I-want-to-decide boss. These managers have a mandate, a budget and impatience. They want to decide.
Advice: Don't steal their thunder. Let them decide! Ask questions like: "What is the next step?", "How do we proceed?", "What is your decision?"

The I-need-assurance boss. These managers are insecure and need help and reassurance.
Advice: Collect Yes-es. Summarize each part and gain acceptance. Then suggest a way forward. "I propose we do this…"

The I-want-more-time boss. These managers take their time. Either they lack the mandate to decide, or they want more facts and data first.
Advice: Ask why they need time and how you can help. Then ask when a decision can be made. This way you get at least a commitment on a time.

Bonus: The I-can't-ever-decide boss
Advice: Give these managers a hug. They need it. Then ask who really decides. Move on.

Reflect on this:

When you want a decision from your boss – how brave are you?

Which decision style do you yourself use most often?

Which decision styles do your bosses use?

"GET ADVICE FROM 200 MEN
THEN DECIDE FOR YOURSELF."
— ALBANIAN PROVERB

Every BEGINNING HAS AN END. *Every* END, A BEGINNING...

My occupational passion is all about human communication. I hope I have given you some food for thought. Consume and digest it. Who knows, you might even become a real joy-spreader (if you aren't already!).

I have a simple mission: I want people to get along and feel good together. Imagine how great it would be if more loved Mondays. Think how much easier it is to lead, sell and collaborate when we feel workplace engagement and motivation. Imagine what fun it is to have fun.

If we become better at communicating with each other, there will eventually be peace on earth. If there is peace on earth, we can save the planet – and ourselves. What a magnificent thought!

The book itself has come to an end. It has taken you not to a finish line but rather to the starting line. Now it's your turn. Fill your workplace with energy, empathy and clarity!

Thanks for reading my mind!

ANTONI LACINAI

Antoni Lacinai is a global speaker wtihin employee engagement, leadership and customer experience. With his 20 communication principles, he speaks at conferences and other meetings by companies and organizations who want to have more fun at work and get better results. He also trains managers and teams in presentation skills, leadership communication, customer communication, trade show skills and how to lead workshops. Added to that, Antoni is a highly esteemed moderator.

This is the 12th book Antoni has written or co-written.

Want more tips and thoughts on how you can get along, have fun at work, lead, sell, collaborate and reach your goals? Visit www.antonilacinai.com where you will find tips, thoughts and videos from Antoni. There you will also find his contact details if you want to book him.

Follow or connect with Antoni on LinkedIn for more insights. His motto: We help each other!

COMMUNICATION IS NOT AN ART.

IT'S A CRAFT.

And like any other craft
you get better
with practice.

A *summery of*
THE 20 SUCCESS FACTORS..

1. You cannot NOT communicate
2. You make people feel what you want them to feel
3. You cannot say what you mean
4. Everyone affects everyone
5. All communication has an intention
6. Better to involve than to inform
7. Analog communication is superior to digital

...OF *communication*

8.   First impressions last
9.   If I am like you, I tend to like you
10. It's better to be interested than interesting
11. Words matter!
12. Keep it simple – not stupid
13. Explain the value, not the features
14. The beginning and the end are most important
15. Three is the magic number
16. Storytelling rules!
17. PowerPoint sucks! – or does it?
18. Your body speaks louder than words
19. Your voice strengthens or sedates
20. Brave people win big

9 789151 942346